Cabeza
de Vaca
NEW WORLD EXPLORER

Cabeza de Vaca

NEW WORLD EXPLORER

by Keith Brandt
illustrated by Sergio Martinez

Troll Associates

Library of Congress Cataloging-in-Publication Data

Brandt, Keith, (date)
    Cabeza de Vaca: New World explorer / by Keith Brandt;
illustrated by Sergio Martinez.
        p.   cm.
    Summary: Describes the life of the sixteenth-century Spanish
explorer who traveled from Florida to Mexico and sought justice and
fair treatment for the Native Americans.
    ISBN 0-8167-2829-1 (lib. bdg.)   ISBN 0-8167-2830-5 (pbk.)
    1. Núñez Cabeza de Vaca, Álvar, 16th cent.—Juvenile literature.
2. Explorers—America—Biography—Juvenile literature.
3. Explorers—Spain—Biography—Juvenile literature.   4. America—
Discovery and exploration—Spanish—Juvenile literature.
[1. Cabeza de Vaca, Álvar Núñez, 16th cent.   2. Explorers.]
I. Martinez, Sergio, 1937-   ill. II. Title.
E125.N9B7   1993
970.01´6´092—dc20
[B]   92-36960

Cabeza de Vaca

NEW WORLD EXPLORER

Young Álvar shaded his eyes from the bright morning sun. The wharf he stood on was noisy, hot, and smelly. There were barrels of fish that had just been hauled ashore. There were huge bunches of bananas, sacks bulging with yams, pineapples, melons, and other brightly colored fruits and vegetables from foreign lands. And there were bamboo cages holding chattering parrots, beady-eyed lizards, monkeys, and other strange creatures.

Álvar Núñez Cabeza de Vaca came to the docks every day. It was the most exciting place in the city of Cádiz. The world seemed to flow into Spain through these docks.

The year was 1500, the beginning of an exciting new century. So many wonderful things were happening! Why, just a few days before, ten-year-old Álvar had seen Captain Christopher Columbus return from his third voyage to the New World. It was a moment printed forever in the boy's mind.

Álvar knew he was destined to live an adventurous life. Adventure ran through his family's history. The family tree included a Knight of the Golden Scarf, a Councilman of the city of Jerez de la Frontera, and a First Lord of Cádiz. And his grandfather, Pedro de Vera, was a famed warrior who had conquered the Canary Islands in the name of Spain.

His mother's side of the family was even more famous. Their name, Cabeza de Vaca, was Spanish for "cow's head." Álvar loved to tell his schoolmates the story of how his family had gotten such an unusual name.

In the beginning of the thirteenth century, the king of Navarre fought a war with North African invaders of Spain called "Moors." The

Moorish army's strong forces in the mountains
of southern Spain had trapped the Spanish army.
Then a shepherd named Martin Alhaja entered
the Spanish king's camp with a plan.

"I have lived all my life in these mountains, tending my flock," said the shepherd. "I am no soldier, but I know how to help your army. There is a very well-hidden pass in the mountains. For many years even I did not know of it. Then, one day, a sheep wandered off.

"I searched and searched until I came upon a narrow pass that the creature had wandered into. Since then I have made my way through this pass many times. But even I have trouble finding it. So I have marked the entrance with the skull of a cow. I can lead your army through this pass."

Martin Alhaja led the Spanish army through the secret pass. In the battle that followed, the Moors were defeated. As a reward, the king of Navarre changed the shepherd's family name to Cabeza de Vaca. From that day on, everyone who heard the name honored the family. And the Cabeza de Vacas became important and wealthy people.

Álvar wanted to begin his own adventures right away. He dreamed of journeys and riches.

Columbus, Cortez, and other explorers had made Spain a powerful, wealthy country. Now the dream of every young Spaniard was to follow in their footsteps and travel to the Indies or to the American continent.

But Grandfather de Vera advised the boy to be patient. "You have much to learn," Don Pedro said. "You must master the art of swordsmanship. You must ride a horse as well as any knight. You must learn navigation, to make your way by sea. You must learn to follow the stars, find water and food anywhere you travel. You must learn how to command others, and how to gain their respect and support. You must learn to use words wisely and well. The world will still be waiting for you when you are grown up."

Álvar took his grandfather's advice seriously, and studied hard. He learned military tactics, navigation, and how to read and make maps. He practiced swordsmanship and the use of firearms. When he was seventeen, he became a cadet in the Jerez Guard. He spent most of his time practicing military skills.

In 1511, when Cabeza de Vaca was twenty-one, he saw his first real action. King Ferdinand of Spain had put together an army to fight in a local war. The battles against the French enemy were fierce and bloody. Cabeza de Vaca went to war a carefree young man. He quickly became a serious adult.

A year later, at the battle of Ravenna, more than 20,000 soldiers died. Cabeza de Vaca was badly wounded, but he was nursed back to health at home. He showed such bravery in battle that he was promoted to the rank of lieutenant. The twenty-two-year-old was next sent to a post near Naples, Italy, where he served with distinction.

In 1513, Lieutenant Cabeza de Vaca returned to Spain as an aide to the Duke of Medina Sidonia. Cabeza de Vaca was in charge of a group of soldiers that kept the peace in the area around Seville. He also served as an assistant to the duke.

The Duke of Medina Sidonia ruled a large territory in southern Spain. He was police chief, tax collector, and principal judge of the area. As the duke's trusted aide, Cabeza de Vaca often did these jobs. His work taught him a lot about human nature. The young officer learned to listen, to say little, to keep careful records, and to show good will while performing his duties.

Cabeza de Vaca was still eager to cross the ocean in search of fame and fortune. But the duke had great confidence in his lieutenant and didn't let him leave. So Cabeza de Vaca served the duke for fourteen years, doing his work well and helping to defeat a number of rebel uprisings in Spain. Then, at last, his government work enabled him to escape from Medina Sidonia.

The duke often sent him on diplomatic missions to the court of Spain's King Charles V. The king was very impressed by the young lieutenant. In 1527, Charles V named him treasurer of an expedition to the New World. Cabeza de Vaca's adventures were about to begin.

The expedition's goal was to set up a colony in Florida. Captain Pánfilo de Narváez was in command of the fleet of five ships. Narváez was also to be governor of the new colony. But the real job of running the Florida colony was placed in the hands of Cabeza de Vaca.

The young man was also ordered to keep the official record of the voyage and the colony. It is through his writings that we know what happened to the fleet under Captain Narváez and to the Spaniards who reached North America.

The fleet sailed on June 27, 1527. Life at sea was miserable. Each ship carried about 120 men, as well as horses, hunting dogs, goats, pigs, sheep, and cattle. The decks and holds were filthy and smelly. Captain Narváez had bought the cheapest, worst ships available. And he was just as cheap with supplies. The captain ate fine cheeses, meats, plenty of vegetables and fruits, pastries, and wine. All others on board had thin soup and a small piece of salted fish four days a week. On the other three days they had a bit of meat or cheese. But their main food was bread.

It took two terrible months to cross the Atlantic and reach the West Indies. As soon as the ships reached Hispaniola (an island now shared by Haiti and the Dominican Republic), 140 men deserted. They cursed Narváez and vowed never to sail with him again. Through it all, Cabeza de Vaca said nothing and did his best to keep peace among the men. He hoped for better conditions in Florida.

In the fall of 1527, the fleet sailed for Cuba. There, over the next few months, Narváez signed on new recruits and bought three more ships, some horses, and supplies. But those were the only good things the captain did. Because he refused to listen to warnings about fierce Caribbean hurricanes, two of his ships sank. With them went sixty men and twenty horses.

Narváez replaced the ships and crew members. Then he made his next mistake. He hired a pilot who swore that he knew every mile of the Caribbean and the coast of Florida. The man turned out to be good at only one thing—lying.

The expedition left Cuba on February 19, 1528, and soon ran aground on a coral reef. The ships were stranded there for fifteen days until a powerful storm freed them. Then the damaged fleet sailed north toward Florida.

Narváez still trusted the pilot. But the man was so bad at his job that it took the fleet two full months to travel only 300 miles. Cabeza de Vaca knew the pilot was a fraud and a fool. The Spaniard was losing faith in Narváez's leadership. He feared the expedition might end in failure and destroy his new career. Most of all, he worried about the safety and lives of the voyagers.

When they finally reached shore, the Spanish set up camp on a beach near a Native-American village. Narváez declared himself governor of Florida. He announced that the land belonged to Spain, and set rules for the Native Americans. They had to convert to Christianity, pay taxes, and accept his word as law.

It was a ridiculous situation. As Cabeza de Vaca wrote, Narváez spoke only Spanish. The Native Americans of the Timucua tribe spoke only their own language. There were no interpreters who spoke both languages. So the only way to communicate was by sign language. It was almost impossible for the Spanish and the Native Americans to understand each other.

On the second day, while the soldiers and the Native Americans were trading trinkets for fish, a soldier noticed something shining in a fish net. It was a piece of gold. Governor Narváez was excited by the news and demanded to know where the gold came from. The Timucua chief saw his opportunity to get rid of these insulting, thieving strangers. He pointed north and said the word *Apalachen.* Then, in sign language, he made the Spanish believe there was a fortune in gold in a province called Apalachen.

Narváez decided to search for the city of gold. He put together a party of 300 men and forty horses. Then he ordered the rest of the men to sail to a big harbor described by the pilot. Narváez was sure he would find the golden city and rejoin the ships in just a few days. So he gave each marcher only two pounds of food.

Cabeza de Vaca felt Narváez was making another big mistake. In his account of the expedition, he wrote, "It seemed to me unwise to leave the ships until they were in a safe port. I told Narváez to consider how many errors the pilot had already made. Furthermore, we had no interpreter to make ourselves understood by the local people.

"Nor did we know what to expect from the land we were entering, having no knowledge of what it was, what it might contain, what kind of people live there, nor in what part of it we were.

"Finally, we didn't have the supplies needed for moving into unknown country. One pound of bread and one of bacon was hardly enough for the journey. My opinion was, we should re-embark and sail in quest of land and harbor better suited to settlement."

Narváez accused Cabeza de Vaca of being afraid. Cabeza de Vaca said he was no coward, and set out to prove it. As he later wrote, "Seeing how utterly unprepared Narváez was for moving inland, I preferred to share the risk with him and his people, and suffer what they would have to suffer. I would much rather expose my life than my good name."

The march north began on May 1, 1528. The Spanish committed many mistakes. They made no effort to hunt or fish. When their food supply ran out, they killed and ate all forty horses, at the rate of one every three days. Otherwise, they lived on the corn or fish they took from Native-American villages they passed through.

Week after week, the voyagers marched on. Only one thing was on their minds: gold. They paid no attention to Florida's rich animal and plant life. Many men fell ill or starved to death because they did not take what nature provided.

At each Native-American village Narváez asked in sign language where to find gold like the piece he had. Each time he was directed north. When he asked for Apalachen, he received the same answer: north. "Is it a big city?" he asked. The Native Americans always said yes.

The truth was, there was no gold or great city in the north. But the Spanish invaders were so cruel and greedy that the Native Americans said anything to get them to leave.

Not every tribe was peaceful. Some met the approaching Spaniards with arrows. The Native Americans were fine archers and warriors. They did not stand still and shoot their arrows or march in rows the way Spanish soldiers did. The Native Americans fought from behind rocks and up in trees. Narváez and his men were confused by these tactics, and many Spaniards died as a result.

By midsummer the surviving Spaniards were ready to end the search for gold. All they wanted to do was reach the harbor where their ships were supposed to be waiting. The soldiers did

not know that the ships had never reached the harbor on the coast of Mexico. The pilot was unable to find it. Instead, the sailors returned to where they had left Narváez and his men. When they found no sign of the expedition, they sailed back to Hispaniola.

Narváez and almost all his companions were
gentlemen who weren't used to working with
their hands. Fortunately, there was one carpenter
and one blacksmith in the group. They taught
the others how to make woodworking tools from
their weapons, sails from their shirts, and rigging
from palm fibers. It took two months of steady
labor to build five rough, open boats. Finally,

at the end of September 1528, they sailed into the Gulf of Mexico.

It was hurricane season during their voyage, and the small boats were tossed around by the blasting winds and huge seas. Supplies were washed overboard. For five days there was no fresh water to drink. At last they sighted land and the mouth of a river, and tried to sail toward it. But the river current was so strong it swept them out to sea.

The boats were about two miles from shore, Cabeza de Vaca wrote, when "we took fresh water from within the sea, because the river ran into the sea with such great violence." This mighty river, able to drive fresh water miles into the Gulf, was the Mississippi. Its fresh water saved the lives of the Spaniards.

Within the two-month voyage, however, three boats—one carrying Governor Narváez—were lost to Gulf hurricanes. The remaining two boats, with eighty weak and despairing men, were driven onto an island now known as Galveston Island, not far from Houston, Texas.

Over the next year, the number of survivors dropped to four. Only Cabeza de Vaca, two other Spaniards, and Estevanico, a Muslim Arab from North Africa, were still alive. Estevanico was a slave who had been captured by the Spanish. His life had been hard, but he was a very intelligent man who learned quickly.

For the next six years, Cabeza de Vaca and his companions lived with a Native-American tribe called the Charruco. The nobleman from Jerez made up his mind to get home alive. To do that, he had to adapt to the place that he was in and to the people who lived there.

At first, Cabeza de Vaca spoke with the Charruco only in sign language. Little by little he learned their language. Once he was able to talk with the tribe, Cabeza de Vaca made a place for himself as a merchant.

The tribes that lived on the coast had a steady supply of seashells, which they crafted into knives and spearheads. They also had reeds and cane for mats, baskets, and other items. What they didn't have were buffalo and deer skins, wood for arrow shafts, animal parts to use for bowstrings, and flint for arrowheads. But the tribes that lived inland did have those things. The answer to everyone's needs was to trade.

Cabeza de Vaca became a traveling salesman for the Native Americans in what is now south Texas. In his words, "The tribes asked me to go about from one part to another to get the things they needed. So, trading my wares I penetrated inland as far as I cared to go and along the coast as much as 120 to 150 miles. This trade suited me well because it gave me liberty to go wherever I pleased. Wherever I went they treated me well and fed me royally. My principle object in trading, however, was to find out how I might get away."

While Cabeza de Vaca was a trader, the other three survivors lived in different Charruco villages. The four men were able to meet only once a year, when the tribe held a festival. Each time, they talked about getting away. Finally, in 1534, the men decided to make their break for freedom.

These men knew nothing about the deserts and mountains of America or the country's great size. But they were survivors who had learned much from the Native Americans. They now knew how to hunt with bow and arrow, fish with spears, find water to drink, and make their own clothing and tools. In many ways they had learned to live off the land. And they were confident that these skills would carry them to safety.

Just as important, the four voyagers had learned to talk to different Native-American tribes, using signs and words. By the time their journey ended, Cabeza de Vaca knew the languages of six different tribes. Estevanico knew many more.

For the next two years, the four walked west. As Cabeza de Vaca wrote, "We always felt certain that going toward the sunset we would find what we desired." Their journey took them across what is now Texas and southern New Mexico, until they reached the Sierra Madre Mountains.

The country was rough and not at all like Spain, with its great roads and cities. But there was a kind of ancient network of trails. Different tribes used them for war, hunting, trading, and moving to new homes when the seasons changed. Cabeza de Vaca had learned about this network while he was a trader for the Charrucos. Now he led his three companions along these trails.

The four travelers lived with different tribes along the way. While they were staying with the Avavares Indians, Estevanico dressed the wound of an injured child. The wound healed quickly and the tribe called him a powerful medicine man. Others came to Estevanico's hut, asking him to cure them of wounds, headaches, and other physical problems.

Estevanico and the other three men did their best to help, and their reputation as medicine men spread. Soon members of other tribes showed up, begging for cures. And they brought payment in the form of animal hides, food, tools, and other things.

The Avavares enjoyed sharing the gifts with their "miracle workers." After a while, they developed a kind of traveling business. The

Avavares sent out runners to tell each tribe when to expect the "healers." Then, while Cabeza de Vaca, Estevanico, and their two companions worked their wonders, the Avavares collected the fees.

The four survivors were happy for the protection of the Avavares, but they wanted to get on with their journey. They finally slipped away under cover of night and joined another tribe, the Maliacones. From their village, Cabeza de Vaca led his men to the village of the Arbadaos. They went from tribe to tribe that way, always heading west or southwest.

Cabeza de Vaca's group crossed the Pecos River and the Rio Grande River. They were the first Europeans to travel through this country. They visited villages where the buildings were made of dried mud called adobe. Here the people had well-kept gardens and fields. Their pottery and tools were well-made and the people were friendly and peaceful.

At last, early in 1536, the travelers reached the western coast of what is now Mexico. There they met a Native American wearing an unusual necklace. It was a leather thong looped through a Spanish sword-belt buckle and a horseshoe nail.

Cabeza de Vaca was excited. As he wrote, "We asked what it was and who brought it. The Indian answered that some men with beards like ours had come with horses, lances, and swords. We asked what had become of these men. The Indian said they had gone to sea."

Cabeza de Vaca also learned there were others like him farther south. So the four survivors walked on. Then, in the spring, they met twenty Spanish soldiers. The soldiers were stunned at the sight of Cabeza de Vaca and his men, who were dressed in animal skins and looked like wild men.

Cabeza de Vaca's happiness at being reunited with his own people soon changed. He was horrified to see how brutal the soldiers were, enslaving and killing peaceful Native Americans. The last eight years had been hard for him. But this kind of cruelty was worse than anything Cabeza de Vaca had seen among the "uncivilized" Native-American tribes.

After resting awhile in Mexico City, Cabeza de Vaca and his three companions boarded a ship for Spain. There he reported his adventures to King Charles V. Then the weary adventurer returned home to Jerez.

But Cabeza de Vaca was not content. All the time he was in America, he dreamed of being back in Spain. Now he dreamed only of the beautiful New World. So he was overjoyed to be appointed Governor of the Province of Rio de la Plata, in Paraguay, South America.

Cabeza de Vaca served there from 1541 to 1543. During that time he tried to create a colony based on justice, honesty, and fair treatment of the Native-American tribes. But those who served under him wanted to enslave the people and make fortunes for themselves. They schemed to get rid of Cabeza de Vaca, and soon succeeded. Cabeza de Vaca was arrested and sent back to Spain in chains. He lived in poverty until his death sometime around 1556.

When Cabeza de Vaca first went to the New World, he hungered for fame and glory and wealth. He found no gold, no jewels, and no glory. Instead, he found a beautiful land that was a treasury of wildlife and many different peoples. He returned from America with a vision of a world in which different people accepted each other. Sadly, this vision was treated with

anger and scorn. But today, those who scorned him are forgotten. And we still remember Cabeza de Vaca with admiration and respect.

INDEX